IMAGES
of England

ROYAL GRAMMAR SCHOOL
HIGH WYCOMBE

The Princess of Wales is greeted by John Prior, Chairman of Governors, and Rowland Brown, Headmaster, on her visit in 1991.

IMAGES
of England

ROYAL GRAMMAR SCHOOL
HIGH WYCOMBE

J.I. Mitchell

TEMPUS

An aerial view of the Royal Grammar School in 1995. The pleasant garden between School House and the Science block was soon to make way for the Language block.

First published 2003

Tempus Publishing Limited
The Mill, Brimscombe Port,
Stroud, Gloucestershire, GL5 2QG

British Library Cataloguing in Publication Data.
A catalogue record for this book is available from the British Library.

ISBN 0 7524 2861 6

Typesetting and origination by Tempus Publishing Limited
Printed in Great Britain by Midway Colour Print, Wiltshire

Contents

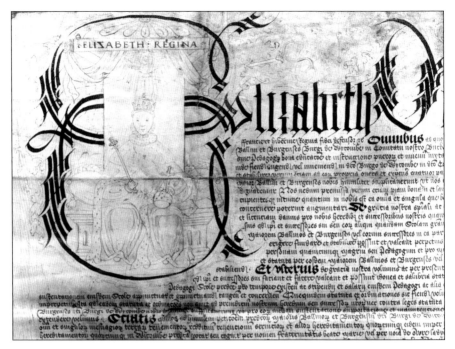

Part of the Royal Charter of 1562, giving authority to 'establish a Grammar School of one Master or Pedagogue for the good education and instruction of boys and youth'.

Acknowledgements

I am indebted to all those who have donated or loaned photographs and given generously of their time as I pestered them for names, dates, identifications or other information I lacked. If any names are missing or if I have misunderstood what I have been told, I hope to be forgiven. I should be grateful to be told of any mistakes of fact.

My thanks to High Wycombe Public Library and the *Bucks Free Press* for permission to use certain pictures; to Cyril Roberts, photographer, for permission to use the 1952 photograph of Tyler's Wood and the 1963 photographs of the new Junior Block; to Associated Newspapers for two photographs; and to Godstowe School for the loan of a photograph. To Mrs S. Bailey for typing the manuscript, Mrs S. Philpot for providing me with a base, and Mrs S. Russell for photocopying facilities, my thanks are also due. The volume *History of the Royal Grammar School, High Wycombe* by L.J. Ashford and C.M. Haworth gives far more information about the RGS up to 1962 than I can supply.

The following have given particular help at various stages of the book's life: R.M. Page, Mrs I. Davies, H. Scott, Mrs J. Pattinson, Mrs H. Prior, I.R. Clark, R.C. File, Mrs E. Smith, A.J. MacTavish, M.W. Cook, J.J.O. Roebuck, Mr and Mrs E.J. Perfect, M. Earl, G.C. Rayner, T.C. Williams, J. Samways, J.P. Edwards, Mrs J. Henderson, Miss H. Munday, Dr R.J. Dosser, Dr J.R. Catch (for information on E.J. Payne), S.B. Gamester, D.G. Stone, P.G. Cowburn, C.C. Tattersall, A.S. Crease, K.D. Keysell, R.G. Ratcliffe, M.C. Ashby, M.G. Jones, Mrs M. Bayley, B. Haunch (for information on B. Rainbow) and D. Willmot.

6

Introduction

Sometime in the twelfth century, the Hospital of St John was founded in the valley to the east of Wycombe itself. It had its own chapel, a Master and brothers and sisters who lived a semi-monastic life devoted to the relief of poverty. Whether a school was attached to the hospital is not known.

The dissolution of religious houses under Henry VIII and Edward VI reached St John's Hospital in 1548; the endowments were confiscated and the Master went to become vicar of Upton. The work amongst the poor was to continue by the founding of almshouses, and some of the money was used to endow a grammar school. The rival claims of school and almshouses were to plague their successors until the twentieth century. However, a schoolmaster, the Revd Mr Wrothe, was appointed at an annual salary of £8 per year. This modest establishment was given a Royal Charter by Queen Elizabeth I in 1562.

The Mastership of the school was poorly rewarded in the succeeding centuries and often combined with another post. When Revd Daniel James died in 1793, no boy was learning Latin, there were no scholars on the foundation and according to Ashford and Haworth's *History of the Royal Grammar School, High Wycombe*, 'but for a few private pupils, the building would have been empty'.

In the nineteenth century, two factors brought about a revival in the school's fortunes: Mary Bowden left £1,000 to be invested to support thirty boys at the school, and Revd James Poulter, curate at the parish church, was appointed Master in 1852. Mr Poulter was a real schoolmaster who devoted all his energies to developing the school and teaching his pupils. The Charity Commissioners reorganized the foundation several times, and an efficient school started to emerge. Mr Poulter organized school cricket matches, played on the Rye, where the burgesses kept their cattle.

A system was started whereby a local examiner was appointed to test the boys' attainment in all the subjects of the curriculum, the first examiner being Revd Francis Ashpitel, vicar of Lane End. At the beginning of the twentieth century the Revd F.L. Nash, also vicar of Lane End, was reporting on English Grammar and Literature, History, Geography, Scripture, French and Latin, while Revd Marchant Pearson examined the school in Physics and Chemistry – a new Science laboratory having been added in 1903, half paid for by the County Council.

Mr Poulter retired in 1879 and his successor, G.J. Peachell, built on the foundations already laid. Within three years a new school had been built behind the old school, which was then demolished, though protests had forced the sparing of some of the medieval remains. The 1883 building provided room for 100 boys, but there were never more than about eighty there at any one time.

A turning point came in 1902 when the Education Act allowed county councils to give grants to independent schools. The Great Western Railway bought land at the back of the school for its new line to London via Beaconsfield, and some of the money was spent on assistant Masters.

Mr Peachell died in 1905 and his successor, G.W. Arnison, from Bridlington Grammar School, quickly established himself. The number of boys increased from fifty-six to 148 by December 1913 and, after long negotiations, the school moved, after over 350 years, to the new site on Amersham Road, into a building designed for around 200 pupils. By the time Mr Arnison retired in 1933 the numbers were up to 330, and further expansion was needed on the new site. During the First World War large numbers of Old Boys and staff joined up, and among the temporary teachers was T.S. Eliot – for one term in 1915.

With the establishment of the school paper, the *Wycombiensian*, in 1905, names became personalities, captured in photographs and in accounts of matches, plays, outings and societies. The prefects' termly day's holiday saw them going off for long walks in the Chilterns or expeditions on bicycles or pony and trap, with stops for refreshment. At Missenden on 9 November 1911, the expedition to Coombe Hill was crowned with 'a glorious tea'. Glorious partly because of the waitress: 'there will always be a warm corner in our hearts for the fair nymph who provided it,' read the report in the *Wycombiensian*.

E.R. Tucker's reign was, like his predecessor's, soon interrupted by international conflict, this time the Second World War. Again boys, staff and Old Boys left to join the forces, and in addition 300 boys came with their teachers from Chiswick High School, until July 1942, to share the buildings on a shift system.

Numbers kept growing, especially at Sixth Form level, and by 1962 there were over 1,000 pupils. A tradition of sending large numbers of boys to university was reinforced after the war, and each year a good number went to Oxford and Cambridge. In the quatercentenary year of 1962 there were nine open scholarships and exhibitions at Oxbridge. The highlight of that year was the visit of Queen Elizabeth II to the RGS, the first of a series of royal visits in the twentieth century.

Like Mr Peachell, Mr Tucker died in harness. His work was continued for the rest of the century by S. Morgan, M.P. Smith, R.P. Brown, D.R. Levin and T.T. Dingle. Numbers have continued to increase, new buildings have arisen and the curriculum was widened to an extent beyond even the examining ability of the polymathic vicars of Lane End. Foreign visits have become comparatively commonplace, and success on the sports fields has blossomed. The first international sportsmen were Ted Woodward and R.E. Syrett for rugby, followed by others in hockey, cricket, basketball, fencing, golf, athletics and shooting.

Old Boys' careers are as varied as there are jobs to go to. A selection of our more famous pupils was exhibited in 2000 at a special evening in the school library. Others not featured in the exhibition include Richard Hickox, the conductor; Roger Scruton, the philosopher and the late Ian Drury, the rock star, though he was not at all happy at school here. Most importantly, the school has attempted to send out into the world boys who have been taught a range of subjects to a high level, and who can take their place as educated young men in whichever sphere they enter.

The future, as ever, is uncertain, but the Royal Grammar School seems well positioned to survive, whatever the storms or shallows that lie ahead.

One
The Old School

When the Hospital of St John was dissolved in 1548, its buildings were put to local use by the burgesses of Wycombe. The refectory, with its Transitional Norman arches, and the chapel were adapted for use as a grammar school. We are not sure exactly how it looked, for the building was altered as well as repaired over the years, but the early prints and photographs show what the Victorians had made of the old structure.

The buildings of St John's Hospital were adapted for use as a Master's house and school, and modified over the centuries. This mid-Victorian print was used as a letter heading. A little girl bowls her hoop while three scholars stand by the arched doorway.

This painting of the rear of the original building shows the gardens and orchard. The school was the Master's house, to which he admitted pupils.

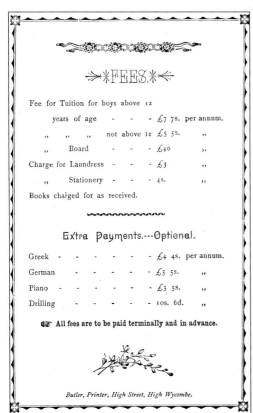

➤ *FEES.* ←

Fee for Tuition for boys above 12
years of age - - - £7 7s. per annum.
,, ,, ,, not above 12 £5 5s. ,,
,, Board - - - £40 ,,
Charge for Laundress - - - £3 ,,
,, Stationery - - - 4s. ,,
Books charged for as received.

Extra Payments.---Optional.

Greek - - - - - £4 4s. per annum.
German - - - - - £5 5s. ,,
Piano - - - - - £5 5s. ,,
Drilling - - - - 10s. 6d. ,,

☞ All fees are to be paid terminally and in advance.

Butler, Printer, High Street, High Wycombe.

This list of charges comes from the early 1890s, tastefully embellished by the printer.

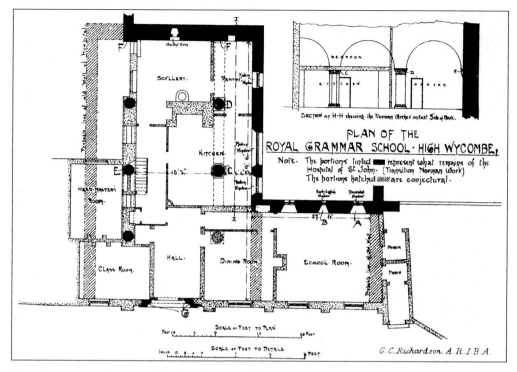

This plan was made upon the demolition of the school building. The portions in black still remain in Easton Street. The first pillar on the left collapsed in 1906. The schoolroom, on the right, might have been the chapel, as it stands east and west.

An early image of the school. Attached to it are four almshouses, which were replaced by E.J. Payne's 1867 almshouses on the opposite side of Easton Street. Below the crenellation is the inscription, 'Schola Regia Grammatica MDLXII'.

E.J. Payne's almshouses were demolished for road realignments. They are pictured here in the late 1960s. Payne was said to have been a pupil of William Burges, architect of Cardiff Castle. He compiled a list, in 1863, of the Masters of the medieval hospital, and of the Masters of the school. Revd Mr Dobson was said by John Aubrey to have been a good schoolmaster, one of his pupils being the poet Edmund Waller (born 1605), author of 'Go, Lovely Rose' and who lived at Hall Barn, Beaconsfield. Other Masters were less distinguished in a post that did not pay well. (Wycombe Library Collection)

E.J. Payne, the son of a gardener, was a scholar of the Royal Grammar School in 1856-57. Here he is seen aged sixteen.

Payne was a remarkable polymath. He was organist at the parish church, and later became the authority on early stringed instruments, especially the *viola da gamba*. He wrote over fifty entries for Grove's *Dictionary of Music*, including that on Stradivarius. He was a Fellow of University College, Oxford; a barrister; author of a history of America and of entries in the *Cambridge Modern History*. His eldest daughter became Professor of Astronomy at Harvard. The photograph is of E.J. Payne while a student at Magdalen Hall, Oxford, (later Hertford College) from where he graduated with First Class Honours.

This photograph of the rear of the original school shows the roofs without the picturesque wavy lines of the painting on page 10.

Some boys peep out of the side entrance to the school in around 1875. The pointed thirteenth-century arch, plastered over a few years earlier, had been discovered and restored to form 'an ornament to the street'.

The ground sloped down towards the road, so a short curved staircase was enough to give entrance to the school garden from upstairs.

Revd James Poulter had revived the fortunes of the Royal Grammar School after his appointment in 1852, but numbers are still small in this 1870s photograph. (Wycombe Library Collection)

Mr Poulter is pictured here shortly before his retirement in 1879, aged seventy-six, with his assistant, F.C. Seaborne, at the left of the photograph. This is the oldest known picture of boys and staff at the school.

A sketch of a possible restoration plan of the building, in a style closer to its medieval origins, yet designed to house a school in a more effective way. Arthur Vernon's plan was not accepted, but he designed both the new 1883 and 1915 buildings.

Two

New Building in
Easton Street

The old buildings had become a liability to the Governors and Masters who lived and worked there. The new Headmaster, G.J. Peachell, was soon to move – in 1883 – into a new building and few in Wycombe regretted the passing of the old one. However, William Morris wrote to urge that it be incorporated into the new building: 'this beautiful work of art [the Norman hall]…in France would certainly have been scheduled as a national monument'. The response was to retain the arches and a medieval wall in front of the new building. Money was always short until the 1902 Education Act, and Mr Peachell struggled to increase numbers and raise standards.

The new building stands proudly back from the road to allow a playground in front. The Wycombe Swan sits in the gable, encircled by the school's name, while a wall post box has replaced the pillar-box seen in earlier views. The new school provided accommodation for 100 boys.

Mr George J. Peachell, a mathematical exhibitioner of St John's College, Cambridge, came as Headmaster in 1879 from St Marylebone Grammar School. He had married the sister of Sir Frederick Bridge, organist of Westminster Abbey, and one of their sons was a talented musician. E.S. Roper, a pupil at the Royal Grammar School in the 1890s, became organist and composer at the Chapel Royal.

Some of the boys pose in front of the new school building in 1883, the old school having been mostly demolished to expose the Norman arches.

The 1883 building, pictured from an upstairs window – perhaps in the almshouses.

A rather overgrown orchard, with the covered playground looking like a miniature Dutch barn.

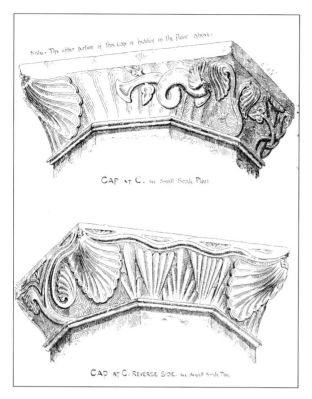

Note - The upper portion of this Cap is hidden in the floor above.

CAP at C. see Small Scale Plan.

CAP at C. REVERSE SIDE. see Small Scale Plan.

After twenty years' exposure to the weather the remains of the Norman building were decaying rapidly. The original carvings had been delicately varied.

Ivy had not helped these gothic windows.

The collapse of one pillar showed the town that matters were in crisis. A glimpse of the almshouses can be seen in the centre of this 1906 picture.

The new Headmaster, G.W. Arnison, led an appeal fund to repair and protect the remains, seen here when the process was nearly complete.

The 1905/06 soccer team. From left to right, back row: Lear, Stephenson, McCoy, Adams (captain), Watson, Stannard, Sanders. Front Row: Appleton, Hervelin, Stone, Birch, Nicholson.

The scene at the laying of the foundation stone at the waterworks shows many of the Royal Grammar School Governors in 1911. From left to right, front row: Alderman Wharton, Alderman Taylor, Alderman Deacon, H. Theed, Alderman Ellis, G.H. Elsom, Dame Frances Dove, Alderman Howland, H.J. Cox, Alderman Stephenson, Alderman Peace's head can be seen on the extreme left, and Arthur Vernon's head just behind Mr Elsom's boater. Vernon was the architect of Watford Grammar School. (Wycombe Library Collection)

Boarders attended the parish church until the school chapel was opened in 1960. The vicars of High Wycombe were, for many years, governors of the RGS.

The opening of the cricket pavilion on ground adjoining the Rye by Revd E.D. Shaw on 20 July 1905. The cost was £47 10s. The match against Mr Shaw's XI was won by the school team, though the vicar, an Oxford Blue, made the top score on either side.

Mr Arnison, pictured here in 1917, started the *Wycombiensian*, the Grey Book – which lists staff and boys – and the Old Boys' Club. His practical attention to detail was demonstrated in the purchase of a donkey, which proved very satisfactory in keeping the cricket turf short.

The RGS in 1908. The staff, from left to right, are: Mr Griffiths, Mr Bartle, Mr Arnison, Mr Threlfall (Second Master), Mr Austin and Miss Douglas. D.J. Watson, to the left of Mr Griffiths, won scholarships to Cambridge where he gained a Double First in Mathematics.

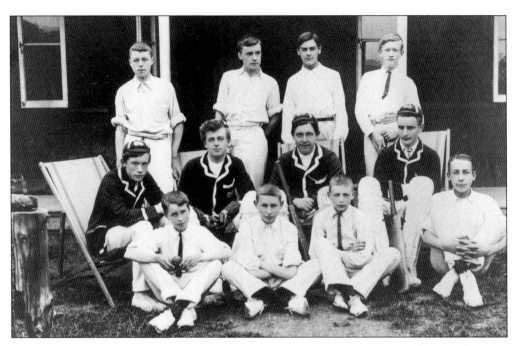

The cricketers of 1907 relax in front of the new pavilion. From left to right, back row: Gillett, Watson, Jackson, Lear. Middle row: Stannard, Stephenson, H.G. Stone (captain), J.C.S. Nutt. Front row: Turner, Butler, Yeoman, Wright.

A Chemistry laboratory had been added in 1903, half the cost being provided by Buckinghamshire County Council, who also paid the Science Master's salary.

Mr Arnison moved Speech Day from the Guildhall and the winter term to the school grounds in the summer. Some of the ladies are sheltering from the sun under their parasols.

Bassetsbury Manor is the background to this 1908/09 soccer group. From left to right, back row: Worley, Weller, Gillett, D.J. Watson (captain), Jackson, Carr. Front row: Richardson, Rutty, Neale, Griffin, Thomas. According to the *Wycombiesian* the season was only 'fairly successful', but the Games Fund was in credit.

The boarders' dining hall in the 1883 building. All the household arrangements were supervised by Mrs Arnison.

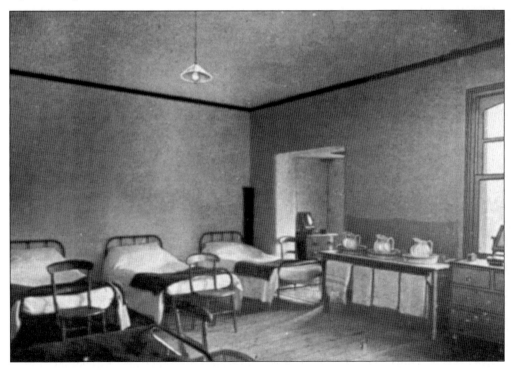

Dormitories were spartan, but perhaps not unusually so for the time. The jugs would be filled with hot water for the boys to wash with.

The Big Schoolroom is, on this occasion, being used by only one class. Under Mr Arnison numbers grew from fifty-six in 1905 to 129 by 1908, when additional rooms had to be hired at Trinity Congregational church. For only five years of his time as Headmaster did the school not exceed its nominal accommodation, he reported in 1933.

In 1905 there were four full-time members of staff, a visiting Music Master and an agricultural instructor. Here, in 1908, there were six full-time teachers. From left to right, back row: Mr Griffiths, Mr Austin, Mr Bartle. Front row: Mr Threlfall, Mr Arnison, Miss Douglas. School entertainments were introduced with songs, recitations and short plays. In 1908 Mr Austin sang 'Father O'Flynn' with 'an extremely Irish accent, and was loudly applauded'. Mr Bartle, in addition to his teaching, was school secretary for many years. Mr Peachell had been his own secretary.

There were 142 boys at the school in 1913, and by then it had been decided to build on a new site rather than on the cramped grounds in Easton Street. Despite strong opposition to, amongst other things, leaving the town centre, the cost and the architect, Mr Arnison announced at Speech Day that the project was definitely going ahead.

The cricket XI of 1911. From the left, back row: Brindley, Avery, Bushell, Richards, Clarke. Middle row: Harvey, Norris (captain), Yeoman. Front row: Spriggs, Chalk, Walton, Hill (scorer). Brindley kept up his cricket in the police force in Ceylon where, in 1932, he made eighty-two not out against the MCC en route to Australia – 'one of the strongest cricket teams that has ever left England'.

Soccer was the main winter sport, though from 1919 rugby was the regular spring term game. In the early days, in all sports, Masters strengthened school teams against older club sides. The 1910-11 soccer team is seen, with mascot, outside the pavilion. Back row, from left to right: Bowler, Rance, Yeoman (captain), Clark, Bushell, Thompson. Front row: Leys, Southcott, Harris, Worley, Harding. The pavilion was taken to the new school in 1915 and was finally replaced after the Second World War.

The annual entertainment included a play, *Vice Versa,* in 1909. F. Youens is second from the right, playing the servant girl, Eliza.

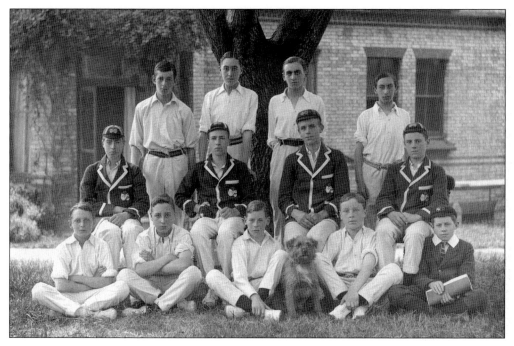

The cricket first XI of 1914, many of whom were soon to be in the Forces. From left to right, back row: E.J. Dormer (Indian Cavalry), T.W. Ballantyne (RAF), C.G. Miles (Sapper), F.S. Berry (Worcestershire Regiment). Middle row: F.J.S. Britnell (Royal Navy and RAF), W.T. Brindley (Oxford and Bucks Light Infantry), W. Line (captain of cricket – Oxford and Bucks L.I.), J.A. Donaldson (Gordon Highlanders). Front row: Thompson, Buggy (Midshipman) R.B. Gotch (RAF – killed in France), R. Donaldson, Downer (scorer).

Copies of this 1910 photograph of *The Rivals* were available for a shilling. From left to right: T.R. Yeoman, D.G. Leys, F. Youens (playing Mrs Malaprop). On the far right, Mr Matthews as Jack Absolute. Of Youens the review said that 'the old lady's failing of mispronouncing words was given with rare point and effect.'

Thomas Samuells in his OTC uniform. He left in 1915 just before the move to Amersham Road. The OTC was formed in 1909 and remained small until the First World War.

Six Masters served in the war. Mr Brand became Second Master in 1919 and remained so until retirement in 1946. F. Norton-Fagge had been founding officer of the OTC. P.L. Jones, appointed in 1916, finally retired in 1964.

32

B.R.P. Wood was 2nd Lieutenant in the City of London Regiment and was accidentally killed instructing men in the use of grenades in 1915.

C.R. Watkins was a private in the same regiment. He was killed in February 1915, the first Old Boy to die in the war. A former fellow pupil said, 'I have lost many friends, as I suppose we all have, but I feel his loss particularly keenly.'

F. Youens won a posthumous V.C. for his actions at Ypres when, despite being treated at the time for wounds, he rushed out to rally his men under German attack. He flung a live grenade out of their trench, but in doing the same to a second grenade it exploded in his hand. He died two days later, aged twenty-two. 'He was admired by everyone for his great bravery,' wrote his commanding officer, 'His was one of the finest acts of bravery in this war.'

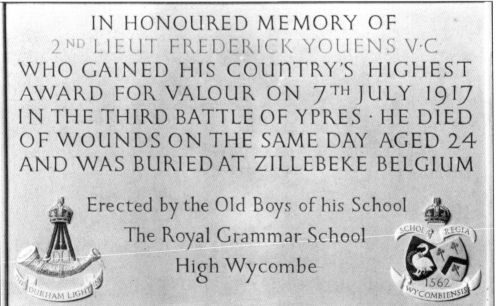

IN HONOURED MEMORY OF
2ND LIEUT FREDERICK YOUENS V·C
WHO GAINED HIS COUNTRY'S HIGHEST
AWARD FOR VALOUR ON 7TH JULY 1917
IN THE THIRD BATTLE OF YPRES · HE DIED
OF WOUNDS ON THE SAME DAY AGED 24
AND WAS BURIED AT ZILLEBEKE BELGIUM

Erected by the Old Boys of his School
The Royal Grammar School
High Wycombe

The plaque erected in Youens' memory in the parish church on 13 December, 1947.

Three

Moving Out of Town

Under Mr Peachell, numbers at the school had not exceeded eighty. In the twentieth century, with new sources of money and a new, energetic Headmaster, numbers increased to such an extent that a new building was necessary. The site at Easton Street was cramped but there was strong opposition to moving a mile up the hill, and to the cost of the new buildings. But thirteen acres were bought and the first sod was cut by representatives of the town. Before the First World War the prefects were given a day's holiday annually, and they were free to explore the surrounding countryside. The new *Wycombiensian* provides cheerful accounts of hikes and waggonette journeys with unwilling ponies. Soon all this was overshadowed by the hostilities with Germany.

In 1914 work began on the new buildings on Amersham Road. The police force can be seen here wielding trowels, with at least one workman enjoying the unusual sight.

The first sod was cut on 6 February 1914 with great enthusiasm. The haystack in the background shows how rural the setting was, and gives some credence to the fears of those who opposed moving so far out of the town.

The foundation stone was laid by the Bishop of Buckingham.

The mayor and corporation walk up to the new site for the laying of the foundation stone. The mace-bearer is J.H. Weston.

The workmen pose in front of the newly-laid foundation stone. The bishop's clerical collar distinguishes him, while the bearded man at the right of the stone is probably the architect, Arthur Vernon.

The ceremony was captured by local photographer, Edward Sweetland, and made into postcards.

Two hymns were sung, 'O God Our Help in Ages Past' and 'Now Thank We All Our God', and the proceedings ended with the National Anthem. Mr Matthews, Second Master in succession to Mr Threlfall, is seen conducting boys and parents. Mr Aleck Stacey accompanied the singing on the cornet.

'In the Faith of Jesus Christ, we place this Stone in the name of the Father, the Son and the Holy Ghost. Amen.' Bishop Shaw had been appointed vicar in 1895 and a governor in the same year. He was Chairman of the Governors until 1921. He became the first Bishop of Buckingham in 1914.

The bishop's chaplain was Revd C.P.S. Clarke, vicar of High Wycombe. The men in this photograph are singing 'God Save the King'.

The buildings soon after completion. On the left, School House is only two storeys high, while there are no wings to the main building. Hamilton Road seems to be a track only.

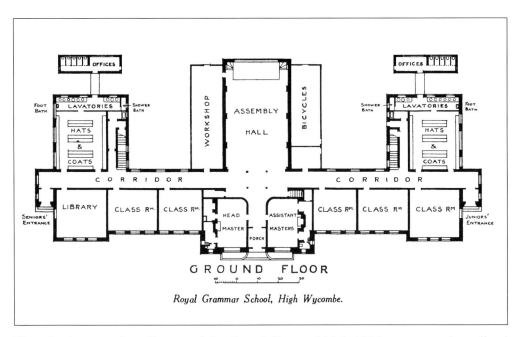

Royal Grammar School, High Wycombe.

The school was not formally opened, but Speech Day on 15 July 1915 incorporated an official opening ceremony. The First World War overshadowed even this momentous occasion. The building was designed for 205 boys.

Mr Arnison was proud that the new school was a Wycombe project: the town council contributed £2,750 of the £20,300 cost, the architect and builder were Wycombe men and the building was equipped largely by Wycombe firms.

The curriculum encouraged practical as well as academic work. The door seen in the far wall now leads to the Matron's room; the rest of the shop is now the Librarian's room.

The dining hall in School House had room for eighty to a hundred and was, in effect, the school's dining room. Mr and Mrs Arnison insisted on neatness and good order.

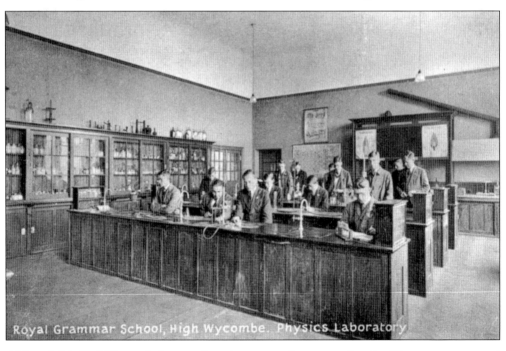

Although labelled 'Physics Laboratory' on this postcard, it was in fact the Chemistry room, and since 1960 it has been the chapel.

The main corridor without fire doors and leading straight into the assembly hall.

Openness and airiness were key ideas in the new building. The hall ended where the present upper library starts.

"HILLSIDE." PRIORY AVENUE.

In previous centuries most schools boarded boys in the houses of individual Masters. At the RGS numbers were small, so the Headmaster's house was the only boarding house. In the early twentieth century increased numbers led to other Masters taking boarders. Here Mr Bartle's house 'Hillside' is advertised as 'well built, the rooms are large and lofty, sanitation and water supply are unexceptional.'

John Axton, a boarder with Revd A.M. Berry, is seen here in his First Form uniform in 1922.

The Arnisons' garden beside School House. The fives courts, just visible to the left of the house, were built as a memorial to those killed in the First World War.

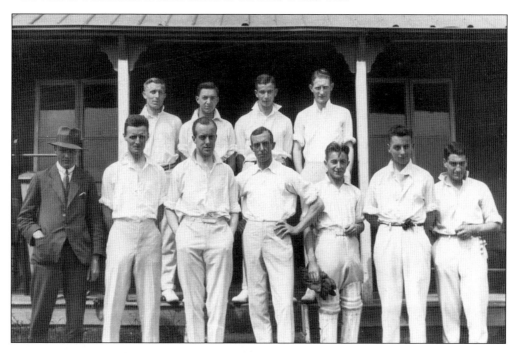

With increased numbers at the school, and Mr Arnison's encouragement, Old Boys' teams were established. Here, from left to right, is the 1926 cricket team. Back row: P.J. Cutler, C.H.N. Locke, R.E. Lacey, E.J. Read. Front row: J.V. Britnell, A. Dodgson, L.F. Watkins, T.H. Redington (captain), C.G. Locke, H.R. Janes, E.G. George. P.J. Cutler gave a school prize for social service. T.H. Redington played football for Wycombe Wanderers and had married Miss Janet Douglas, Languages Mistress at the RGS, in 1910.

Having separate Physics and Chemistry laboratories was a luxury the school had not previously experienced. The Physics laboratory is now used for Information Technology.

ROYAL GRAMMAR SCHOOL, HIGH WYCOMBE.

REPORT FOR TERM ENDING *17th December*, 1920.

Name *Layne, T. E.* Age_____ years_____ months.

Form *V. b.* of *30* boys. Average age of Form *15* years *1* months.

Height *5* ft *9½* in. Weight *9* st. *0* lbs. Chest *31½* in.

FORTNIGHT	1	2	3	4	5	6	TERM.	EXAM.	FINAL.
FORM ORDER.	18	15	14	16	10	10	13	12	14

SUBJECT.	ORDER. TERM.	EXAM.	REMARKS.	
Scripture.	11	18		4. 6. S.
English.	18	19	Has made good progress	J.E.J
Writing & Spelling.		17	Writing weak Spelling fair	
History.	27	20	Fair improving	
Geography.	5.	13.	Very fair.	
Latin.				
French.	27	26	Very weak.	A.M.
German.				
Mathematics.	2	1	Very good.	
Science.	14	10	Taking satisfactory progress	
Nature Study.				
Drawing.	8	3	V good. Is rapidly improving	
Modelling.				
Woodwork.				
physical Training.				

Attendance (Whole days count as 2 attendances)   Absent_____   Late_____

Conduct. *Very satisfactory*

If he works hard and makes considerable improvement in English subjects and French, he should qualify for a School Certificate. G. W. A.

Form Master *J. Scotney B.Sc.*

Head Master, **G. W. ARNISON, M.A.**

Next Term will begin at 9.30 a.m. on *Wednesday, 19th January 1921*. Boarders return on the previous day.

T.E. Layne's Christmas term report in 1920, beautifully headed by his form Master, J. Scotney BSc.

The OTC in 1920 with Captain F.H. Robinson, the officer commanding.

F.H. Robinson succeeded Mr Matthews (who had gone to be Headmaster of Southwell Minster Grammar School) as Geography Master and O.C. of the OTC. His second in command, J.E. John, was a much-admired English Master.

The staff in 1926. From left to right, back row: S. Cook, J.E. John, G.A. Grant. Middle row: F.R. Eady, C.G. Harris, S.A. Watt, F.H. Robinson, A. Marti, J.A. McQueen. Front row: P.L. Jones, Revd A.M. Berry, H.G. Brand, G.W. Arnison, W.J. Bartle, J.A. Hurn, J. Sumpter.

George Grant was Art Master for many years. He also founded the Hobby Club, which provided opportunities for its members – more than half the school by 1929 – to attend lectures (often illustrated by lantern slides), to go on visits and to hear members' lectures. In 1929 they visited the Royal Mint and the Tower of London, the Science Museum, Cadbury's chocolate factory, the British Museum and Southampton Docks. Sixty-nine boys went camping for three weeks in Jersey.

Royal Grammar School, High Wycombe.

Because of lack of money, the school did not own the ground between the Amersham Road and the gate. The entrance is opposite the Senior boys' door, not the main, central door.

The strong tradition of school drama was fostered by Revd A.M. Berry as producer. G.A. Grant was set designer and Mrs Arnison and her daughter made up the actors. The farcical comedy *The Adventure of Lady Ursula* was given in December 1931, as a piece of light relief. S.N. Blacklock, in the centre as Lady Ursula, was highly praised.

49

Mr Berry retired in 1933 and became vicar of Willen, near Bletchley. Here, in his 1928 production of *King Lear*, G.V. Seymour (as Kent) is in the stocks, with K.T.B. Scott (Regan) pointing scornfully. According to the *Wycombiesian*, Scott's performance 'was of outstanding merit'.

Lear is flanked by his daughters. The Fool, G. St. J. Larkin, who gave 'a good account of himself', is identified by his distinctive tights. Mr Berry's final production was *Hamlet*, with S.N. Blacklock in the title role. The *Wycombiensian* called the production the crowning triumph of Mr Berry's dramatic efforts. Proceeds from the plays went to the Games Fund – over £40 on this occasion.

J.C. Milner (known as Tiny), Lord Cottesloe and G.W. Arnison at Speech Day, 1933. Lord Cottesloe, Lord Lieutenant of Buckinghamshire, had presented prizes on Mr Arnison's last Speech Day as Headmaster.

The 1927 soccer team. From left to right, back row: Craven (scorer), Underhill, Carr, Bull, White. Middle row: Wells, Horley, N.R. Hawes (captain), Perfect, Dean. Front row: Spriggs, Clark. Soccer did not survive the 1930s as a school sport.

The Old Boys raised sufficient money to buy Mr Arnison a Rover car. Here he and Mrs Arnison, at their new house at Flackwell Heath, appreciate the gift. Mr Arnison retired aged fifty-eight, but continued to take an active interest in the school until his death in 1965, aged ninety. He seems to have been universally admired.

The 1932 soccer team. From left to right, back row: Wingrove, Ray, Britnell, Humphries, Peatey. Middle row: Emery, Essex, A.A. Coventry (captain), Fountain, Reynolds. Front row: Blacklock (linesman), Sears. F.W. Essex had a successful career in the Colonial Service in Sierra Leone, British Guiana and, finally, Rhodesia. Alan Coventry came back to the school as a Master, but died aged only thirty-nine.

Four

E.R. Tucker and Another Great War

Mr Arnison retired, feeling in need of a rest after twenty-eight years as Headmaster. His successor was another Classicist who inherited a well-run school with a small Sixth Form. Mr Tucker resolved to build the Sixth Form and to gain recognition for the school at Oxford and Cambridge. After the setback of the Second World War, this work was resumed, but the early successes were recognised by his election to the Headmasters' Conference in 1943.

The Governors again chose a young man as Headmaster: E.R. Tucker was thirty-one in 1933. He had been Second Master at Pocklington School in Yorkshire and before that Classics Master at Bemrose School, Derby. He took over a school of 330 boys and sixteen Masters.

The 1934 soccer team won all its inter-school games. Back row, left to right: Hawes, Boddy, Harding, Turner. Middle row: Lee, Balls, Essex (captain), Oakeshott, Uden. Front row: Griffin, Edwards, Gomm.

Godstowe School graciously took in a number of boarders on the night of 1 November 1935, when fire gutted the boarding house.

A rare view of the boarding house before the fire of 1935.

The new three-storey house seen from the Headmaster's garden.

W.D. Yeoman, third from left, seems to be leading the field in this 1938 photograph. The 1905 pavilion had been moved from the Rye up to the new field in 1915. (Copyright *Bucks Free Press*)

The 1939 lst XI. From left to right, back row: Baldwin, Winter-Taylor, West, Lear, Mugliston, White, Perfect. Front row: Witney, Timpson, P. Thorne (captain), Hughes, Hazell. D.R. Witney later became Headmaster of King Edward VI Grammar School in Louth.

The first important addition to the buildings was the Gym Block in 1930. It provided cloakrooms and four classrooms as well as a gymnasium. At the far right of the picture can be seen the signals hut. In 1937 two wings were added to the front of the school, and the assembly hall was extended, almost doubling its length and adding a proper stage for the first time.

The gymnastics display at the 1937 Speech Day. The original end of the hall can be seen. (*Bucks Free Press*)

1938 boxing finalists. From left to right, back row: Yeoman, Hoare, Oakeshott, J.P. Lord, Wilkes, Thorne, B. Smith, Harris, Kohnshtam, Thornton. Middle row: D.E. Lord, Taylor, Vaughan, C.E.C. Eastman, R. Pattinson, Stevens, Birch, Mansbridge. Front row: Clark, Piercey, Pocock (younger), Rhodes, Tanner, Robertson, Pocock (elder), Carter.

The hall before 1937. Photographs of the Old Boys who died in the First World War are on the walls, and the bronze war memorial is between the flags on the right-hand side. Thirty-eight Old Boys and two Masters were killed.

The Art room seen in the late 1930s.

Senior boarders in 1939. From left to right: Ward, Castle, J.O. Roberts (staff), Grover, Collins, T.F. Rayner, Haynes, Rhodes, J.K. Prior, Barrett. J.O. Roberts later moved to Hardye's Grammar School, Dorchester. Rhodes became a major in the Second World War, where he was awarded the MC.

The first recorded school trip was to Paris in 1939. Here S. Morgan (staff), L.A. Dickson, P.W. Ward and N. Polmear (staff) are seen round a flagpole; the exact location is unknown.

P.W. Ward poses on the Gym Block. An enthusiastic group of boarders developed their own photographs and were eager for interesting subjects!

The cadets at OTC camp in 1937 are smartly turned out, but the low numbers for such a school were criticized. As had happened a generation earlier, the war changed attitudes to the Corps.

J.K. Prior leads the OTC at the General Inspection on 13 June 1940. Mr Prior was for many years Chairman of the Governors. The saluting base was the Headmaster's private entrance a little further along Hamilton Road.

The 1941 cricket lst XI. From left to right, back row: Clark, Jones, Whiting, Redrup, McQueen (younger). Front row: Long, L.H. Smith, Barnard, Witney, Hazell, McQueen (elder). Priest, in front, was scorer. The McQueens' father taught Modern Languages.

A peaceful view, with well-cared-for grounds on both sides of Hamilton Road.

Peter Thorne outside his home at Land End. He wrote in a letter to his fiancée about 'a priceless one of me with School cups and things at the front door'. An athlete and a scholar, he went to Jesus College, Cambridge on an English Exhibition. He joined the RAF as a pilot and was reported as missing, presumed killed, in February 1945. His widow presents an annual Thorne Prize for English in his memory.

Games continued, despite difficult conditions. The 1944 cricket lst XI, from left to right, back row: -?-, -?-, Lochhead, Goldsmith, -?-, -?-. Seated: Roith, Lang, Shillabeer, -?-, Williamson. Scorer: M.W. Warburg.

The JTC (Junior Training Corps) band in front of the main entrance in 1944. By then there were 300 boys in the JTC – successor of the OTC – and 230 in the Air Training Corps.

The JTC band marching in the High Street during War Weapons Week in 1944. The Drum Major is Eric Lewis. Front row, left to right: Tony Duckering, Roger Banham, David Tanner, Sid Leach.

Five

Post-War Recovery

Changes brought about by the 1944 Education Act led to the school becoming Voluntary Controlled, and the expansion in numbers continued. Two new boarding houses opened and, for the first time, Saturday morning school was abandoned.

Lieutenant Ian Fraser won the Victoria Cross as commander of a midget submarine. On 31 July 1945, against almost impossible odds, he succeeded in blowing up a Japanese cruiser. The approach and withdrawal entailed a passage of eighty miles through water that had been mined by both the enemy and ourselves, past hydrophone positions, over loops and controlled minefields, and through an anti-submarine boom.

H.G. Bass, Head Prefect, presenting an engraved cigarette and cigar box to Lt. Ian Fraser VC, 18 December 1945. Air Vice-Marshal Langford Sainsbury was principal speaker. F. Youens' mother was present. Their names are honoured in the present boarding house.

A Scout troop was set up during the war, primarily for boarders. Here they are on camp around 1950. Mrs Iris Davies and her son can be seen seated next to the boy with the bobble hat; her husband, M.M. Davies, is opposite her, with his back to the camera.

An Old Wycombiensians' dinner believed to be at the Connaught Rooms, London, probably in 1948. Left hand side, from the front: Messrs. S. Hands, Hawley, Bunce, J. Walter, Church. Next row, from the front: Messrs. Lee, Harley, Barnard, -?-, -?-, J. Hands, Rogers, Butler, -?-, Rendall. Third row, from the front, backs to the camera: Messrs. L. Jenkins, P. Ward, B. Collins, D. Barnett, T. Jenkins, Lewis. Fourth row, from the front: J. Castle, T. Rayner, Barnett, G. Rayner, Leeser. Ranged along the back from left to right are, fourth from the left: Mr Brand, -?-, Mr Arnison, Mr Tucker, Revd A.M. Berry.

School House in 1951 or 1952. Ordinary or colours blazers were only worn in the summer term. In the centre sit Matron, Mrs Tucker, Mr R. Howard and Miss Angela Tucker. Mr Peter Draper, who lent the photograph, is on the back row, third from the left. Mr Howard became Head of English at Royal Latin School, Buckingham.

Uplyme was opened as a boarding house in 1948. Mr H. Scott was the first Housemaster and he was succeeded by Mr Mervyn Davies. During the war the house had been used by Ingersoll. The huts from those days were later used as the Junior School, and still survive as C.C.F. (Combined Cadet Force) rooms.

Uplyme boarders, with Mr Davies, around 1950. On his right is the matron, Miss MacIntire. On his left, Mrs Iris Davies who taught Science both at the RGS and later at Lady Verney High School.

Tylers Wood opened later in 1948, with Mr R. Pattinson as Housemaster. The house had belonged to the distinguished scientist Sir William Ramsay, Fellow of the Royal Society and Professor of Chemistry at University College, London, who was awarded the 1904 Nobel Prize for Chemistry, and was an honorary member of nearly every scientific academy in the world. Some of his scientific instruments were given to the RGS on his death in 1927.

Some extensions were made to the house to equip it more effectively for boarding purposes. The house closed and the site was sold for housing in the 1980s. After years of neglect, Tylers Wood was demolished and a new house built on the site.

Tylers Wood residents in 1952. From left to right, back row: Fryer, -?-, Robertson, Hickey, Rankin, -?-, -?-, Aikens, Gowan. Second row: Gaffoor, Kay, Minter, Lacey, Owen, J. Edwards, Woods, -?-. Third row: Johnston, Sinnatt, Abdallah, Mr Horace Johnson, Mr R. Pattinson, Miss Blythe, M.J. Edwards, Hussein, Gordon. Front row: -?-, -?-, Scott-Kiddie, -?-, Mardell, -?-, -?-. (Photograph courtesy of Cyril Roberts)

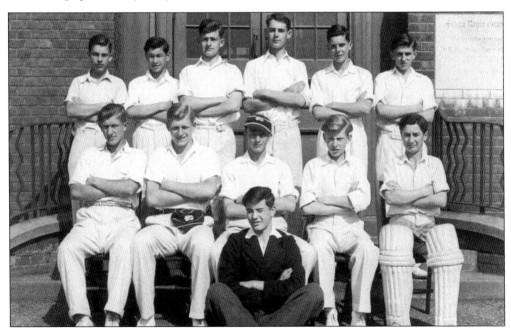

The 1947 cricket season was notable for the glorious summer weather, and for the school's fielding three regular school sides. The captain, wearing his cap, was R.H. Tunmer; to his left is J.E. Woodward, who played rugby for England – the school's first international sportsman. The wicket keeper, extreme right, seated, is I.S. Lochhead, whose record for the season was: 'Caught 10, stumped 12'. His innocent face lured many to their doom: 'the team always felt that he was so sorry to stump an opponent but that was the call of duty he had to obey'.

The staff cricket team. From left to right, back row: A. Coventry, H. Thomas, 'Ginger' Jones, M. Davies, F. Eldridge, T. Hood, R. Howard. Front row: C. Haworth, H. Johnson, E.R. Tucker, S. Morgan, J. Roberts. The staff beat the school by fifty runs.

The best innings of the 1952 season was by I.T. Johnston, an occasional member of the XI and not shown here! From left to right, back row: Brooks, Crump, Emmins, Elliott, Pursey, Dixon. Seated: Hawkins, Wing, M. Bridges (captain), Walker, Ashby. P. Draper was scorer.

The Mikado and Katisha listen to pleas for mercy. From the left, B.C. Stevens, A.J. Sadler, D.J. Crump. The Mikado is M.S. Matthews and the elderly lady Katisha is F.J.R. Hobson.

Bernarr Rainbow was the first full-time Music Master. He introduced annual Gilbert and Sullivan performances. When he left the RGS, the *Wycombiesian* expressed the view that 'he leaves to his successor a musical school and a musical heritage that is all of his own making. The pleasure and delight which he has given to so many boys will never be forgotten'. This photograph shows him in his Doctor of Letters robes after he had left the school.

Tennis was encouraged by the Headmaster, as were all team games. The first team of 1952 was, from left to right, back row: Monks, Johnson, Wheeler. Seated: Hester, Ashby, Kipping, Osborne.

On 19 December 1949 the staff rugby team gave its last performance. From left to right, back row: 'Ginger' Jones, A. Duckering (Old Wycombiesian), J. Tucker. Middle row: P.L. Jones, L.T. Hollingworth, J. Cowan, W. Rees, H. Scott, T.V. Shepherd, P.D. Fry (Old Wycombiesian). Front row: J. Edwards, A. Coventry, C. Haworth, E. R.Tucker, R. Pattinson, M. Davies, G. Young. They lost 6-0 to the school first XV.

The rugby second XV won twelve games and lost one game in 1953-54. R.C. Pilgrim was captain. Back row, far left next to the linesman, is F. Hawkins, an all-round sportsman who founded Hawkinsport in High Wycombe. Back row, second from the right is R.F. Sainsbury, later Bishop of Barking. Front row, second from the right is G.D.B. Jones, who became the first Professor of Archaeology at Manchester University.

The Royal Navy C.C.F. petty officers and leading seamen in 1955.

The cricket pavilion was opened in 1956 as a memorial to Old Boys who had been killed in the Second World War.

The captain of the cricket first XI, F.E.J. Hawkins, scored 647 runs in the 1956 season and performed twenty-five stumpings. His highest score was ninety-one. From left to right, back row: Dawe, R.C. Jones, Todd, Smithers, Edwards, Pettifer. Seated: Wright, Harvey, Hawkins, Squires, Briden. D.P. Ketch was scorer.

The first major building after the war was the Science school, opened in 1960. Not only did this greatly expand facilities for teaching Physics, Chemistry and Biology, it also made more room in the rest of the school for Art, History and a new chapel. A new Science library helped reduce overcrowding in the school library. The Science block had to be altered in 1998 because of structural problems.

Six
400 Years of the
Royal Grammar School

There were 960 boys in the school by 1960, and again new buildings were called for. First the Science block and then the new Junior School were built in front of the main buildings. The design was controversial and noise from the main road an increasing problem, but the accommodation was welcomed with enthusiasm. The highlight, however, was the visit of Queen Elizabeth II to the town and school.

Michael Eaton, then Head of Art, drew this impression of what was to become the Queen's Hall and Junior block in 1960. At this time it was the intention that the fine views of the old school should not be hidden behind the new.

Mr Tucker had long been a lay reader in the Church of England. Here he is seen in the new chapel, with Revd A.J. Skipp, School Chaplain and Old Boy. The furnishings of the chapel were designed and donated by Old Boys.

The new cricket pavilion, which replaced Mr Arnison's 1905 pavilion, cost about £5,000. The 1960 1st XI was, from left to right, back row: Barlow, Bowler, Stratford, Punton, Dronfield. Front row: Riley, Miller, C.D. Waller (captain), Simpson, Fountain, Holdship. A Seale was scorer.

Every ten years a photograph is taken of the Classical Sixth Form. In the 1961 photograph, from left to right, back row: Farmer, Sleigh, Wood, Taylor, Green, Mahoney, Buckley, North. Middle row: Marshall, Evans, Palmer, Durham, Hamilton-Eddy, Bristow, Walker, Macready, Garner, M.G. Smith, Chandler. Seated: Helena Ellis, Messrs. Curry, Male, Tucker, Haworth, Benson, Pursey, E.W. Burrows. Helena Ellis was the only full-time girl pupil in the school's history – no other local school at that time offered the full classics course. She won an open award at St Anne's College, Oxford, and later married an Old Boy.

Mervyn Davies, Head of German and Housemaster of Uplyme, was also a much loved form Master of Junior forms. Here he is with 2E in 1961.

The first royal visit to the school took place on 6 April 1962, to mark the quatercentenary of the Royal Charter, seen here being admired by, from left to right: W.B. Watmough, P.L. Jones, W. Clark, A.C. Hills and S. Morgan. (Associated Press)

Her Majesty the Queen shakes hands with G.W. Arnison. Between them can be seen Alderman Baker, P.C. Raffety and Alderman Mary Towerton.

Mr Tucker's pride in the occasion is clear as he escorts the Queen. Behind is the Head Boy, David Stratford. On the far right is R.P. Clarke, Chairman of the Governors.

Her Majesty was met by the Lord Lieutenant, Sir Henry Floyd. Then, from left to right, are Lord Curzon, Chairman of the Bucks Education Committee; F.J. North, Chief Education Officer for Bucks; Alderman R.P. Clarke; Mr Tucker; Mrs Tucker; David Stratford.

A.C. Hills, Senior English Master, introduces the Queen to some of the RGS historical material. Her Majesty signed a specially bound copy of the Grey Book.

In those more disciplined days a single rope was enough to contain the crowds in front of the canteen. The Scout hut is behind Mr Tucker's head.

The tablet that is now in the foyer of the Queen's Hall is unveiled, to everyone's delight. Neither hall nor foyer was complete at that time.

Scaffolding provided a grandstand for some as the Queen was driven away from the school. Soon the main block would be hidden from the road, and the Juniors would leave the Uplyme huts for new classrooms.

After the Queen's departure, the Headmaster is able to relax.

By 1963 the finishing touches were being put to the new building and the new 'quadrangle'. Originally there were rather ineffective fountains below the bollards. Mr R.P. Brown had them removed and replaced by flowerbeds. (Cyril Roberts)

The Royal Coat of Arms was rescued from Hartwell church, near Aylesbury, and placed at the head of the stairs to the Queen's Hall.

A sparkling new Junior classroom, though the desks did not stand up to the hard wear that the old cast-iron framed desks could endure. (Cyril Roberts)

On the day of the Queen's visit, E.R. Tucker could look back on a long and distinguished career. However in July he suffered the loss of his wife, who died suddenly one Sunday afternoon. (Associated Press)

Two years later, Mr Tucker himself died suddenly, a year before his planned retirement. In his memory this Tucker Memorial Room was built as a Sixth Form common room. It is now the Careers room

In 1964 the school tennis team won the Youll Cup by beating Charterhouse in the final at Twickenham. From left to right, front row: -?-, P.J. Moores, M.E.J. Panter, P.B. Farmer, D.M. Davies. C.M. Haworth is to the right behind Davies.

An aerial view taken in the 1960s after the completion of the Junior block and new canteen – now the Sixth Form common room.

A guard of honour welcomed Mr H.S. Magnay, former Chief Education Officer for Liverpool, to the 1966 Speech Day. From left to right: A.J. MacTavish (with sword), Mr Magnay, L. Arnold, C. Clark, G. Spittle.

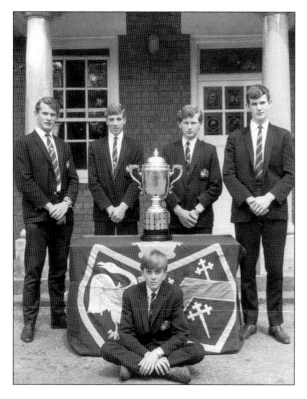

Mr MacTavish started rowing at RGS. In 1966 the lst IV won the Reading Junior Maiden Fours. From left to right are: Farmer, Oliver, Helyar (captain), Selwyn-Jones. In front: C. Rutherford (cox). (Copyright *Bucks Free Press*)

Seven
The Turbulent Sixties and Seventies

On Mr Tucker's death in July 1964, Sam Morgan became acting Headmaster and W. Clark his deputy. They ran a very tight ship. Grammar schools were out of favour and the new Headmaster, M.P. Smith, fresh from school selection battles in Liverpool, was active in promoting the values of selection. In Buckinghamshire, the raising of school leaving age to sixteen meant that pupils were transferring to Secondary schools at age twelve, so that the last first form made up of eleven-year olds for nearly twenty years entered in 1973.

By the 1960s there were over 1,000 boys in the school and whole school photographs were impractical. A section of the Junior School in 1967 shows staff, from left to right: C.M. Haworth, G. Browning, J.C.S. Weeks, M.M. Davies, A.D. Leggett, S. Morgan, M.P. Smith (Headmaster), L.T. Hollingworth, W. Clark, T.V. Sheppard, B. Leighton-Jones, M. Coldham, K.D. Millican, -?-, P.A. Taylor, R. Farrell, R. Palmer, E. Jones.

Malcolm P. Smith was appointed Headmaster in 1965, having been Head of two schools previously. An Old Boy of Manchester Grammar School with a First in Modern Languages, he was keen to maintain the high standards established by his predecessors. A particular hobby was bookbinding – examples of his work are on the shelves behind him.

Sam Morgan, who had been appointed in 1930 to teach Geography, succeeded H.G. Brand as Second Master in 1946. He retired in 1973 to general regret, his fierceness towards the evil doer never detracting from the respect and affection felt for him by the school.

The staff soccer team started in 1968. This picture from 1975 shows, from left to right, back row: M.W. Cook, D.R. Chamberlain, R.M. Page, P.M. Gibson, P.G. Raymond, M.J. Moffatt, D.G. Stone. Front row: S.B. Gamester, K.A. Hillier, I.J. Wilson, R.J. Dosser.

In the nineteenth century, boys bathed on the Rye. A swimming pool on school premises was mooted fifty years before the present pool was opened in 1965.

The 1967 Old Boys' Dinner at the Red Lion, High Wycombe. The picture includes M.M. Davies, M.P. Smith, J.K. Prior, G.C. Rayner, S. Morgan, R. Pattinson and Revd A.J. Skipp.

With the advent of the Queen's Hall, the 'old' hall was used as a gymnasium, with much of the stage blocked off by a partition. Under the stage the model railway club flourished for many years.

One of Mr Morgan's retirement gifts was a flight over High Wycombe from Booker airfield. From left to right: Mrs Louise Morgan, M.P. Smith, S. Morgan.

The First IV at Cambridge. From the left: A. Cardy, A. Tyler, M. Sinden, T. Airey; I.A. Blyth, Master in charge, coxed. As well as his responsibility for rowing, Mr Blyth was the driving force behind staff revues, in succession to K.A. Hillier.

Until Mr Tucker's death, the Headmaster had been also Boarding Housemaster. Revd A.J. Skipp succeeded to the latter post in 1964, remaining Housemaster until his retirement in 1982. This photograph shows a group of his boarders. From left to right, back row: Dutton, -?-, Friend, -?-, Morris, Perring, Hopcraft, Jenkins. Second row: Edwards, Sansome, -?-, Causdale, -?-, Mrs J. Pattinson, Boreham, Carpenter, Reid, Gwenlan, -?-, -?-. Third row: McEwan M. Coburn, Appleton, Pillidge, A.J. Skipp, D. White-Taylor, -?-, M.A. Coburn, -?-. Front row: Sullivan, -?-, Fuller, Read.

S.B. Gamester coached the 1975/76 under-15 rugby team: they suffered only three defeats. From left to right, back row: Dean, Molesworth, Goodwin, Stott, Scott-James. Second row: Madgwick, Corfield, Barrett, Coburn, Shakespeare, Tregunna. Front row: Buckingham, Vladar, Speed, Morgan (captain), Connor, Billig, Morrish.

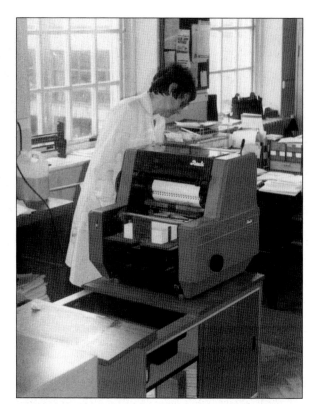

In 1973 the Junior library moved to what is now Room 1, and the Resources centre was set up by the librarian, K.A. Hillier. The first technician was Mrs A. Worley, seen tending the lithograph machine. Much that had been printed professionally could now be produced in school to a high standard. The Computing centre now occupies the room.

E.J. Perfect, who introduced Russian to the school, led a party to Leningrad in 1978. In the background is the cruiser *Aurora* – a key player in the 1917 Russian Revolution. On the far right is Wayne Nash, while in the centre, with scarf, is a Russian schoolboy. The Russians were not allowed into the visitors' hotel, neither could they invite the English into their homes.

On Mr Morgan's retirement, Mr R. Pattinson, left, became Deputy Headmaster. He is seen here with M.M. Davies, centre, talking to parents on Speech Day.

The express form which took 'O' level in four years instead of in five was phased out in 1973 when boys began arriving at the school at age twelve rather than eleven. Distinctions in the boys' abilities were hidden by calling forms by Masters' initials. 4G in 1979 was S.B. Gamester's form. From left to right, back row: MacDonald, Bleiker, Hawkins, Gillingham, Makins, Rixon, Norrish, Hutton, Barr, Madgwick, Sharp. Second row: Lee, Wilkinson, Turnbull, Leonard, Curzon, Studer, Desimone, Taylor, Ashdown, Petersen. Front row: Griggs, Giles, Pook, Willis, Glover, Plane, Amos, Mehmood.

The 1979 tennis team was captained by M. Coburn, front row, second from left; the Masters in charge were Mr M. Earl and Mr S. Grundy.

As numbers continued to grow, terrapin huts were erected to supply temporary classrooms. At the time this photograph was taken in 1986, the new canteen was soon to be joined to the Sports Hall and canteen, and the old kitchens to the left of the picture were to be demolished.

The 'Culture Vulture' club arose out of the Film Society in 1974. Here Junior Vultures are high above London in the Millennium Eye in 2000.

Dennis Smith was appointed Head of the Junior School in 1971, in succession to L.T. Hollingworth. An Art Master, he was fully involved in school drama. In his farewell production of A *Midsummer Night's Dream*, the rude mechanicals were played by members of staff. P.G. Cowburn advertises the attractions of the production to the school.

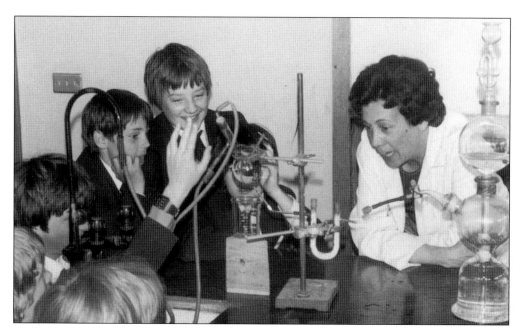

Here Mrs M. Campbell has the attention of her Chemistry pupils in the now middle-aged Science block.

J.R. Learmonth, Head of Physical Education, trained the 1981/82 under-16 basketball team. From left to right, back row: Treadwell, Topping, Carter, -?-, -?-. Front row: Morrish, Knox, Britton, Marsland, Drewett.

The CCF's officers in this 1980 group are, from left to right, middle row: H. Munday, A.J. Sollars, C.P. Smaje, R.H. Boutland, M.G. Mill.

There had been a jazz band in the 1950s, but this band started in 1979 under the direction of Mr B. Trafford, seen in the white shirt, below the portrait of G.W. Arnison. Dr Trafford is now Headmaster of Wolverhampton Grammar School.

Eight
New Buildings and Wider Horizons

With the purchase of school minibuses and opportunity for foreign travel ever expanding, the 1980s and 1990s saw sports teams going as far as South Africa, and Foreign Language and History trips becoming commonplace. With wider horizons, however, the essentials of hard work and high standards have been kept clearly in view.

The old canteen, actually a post-war building, pictured shortly before its demolition. Staff sat at each table of eight and grace was said before meals until the introduction of a self-service system.

S.B. Gamester and D. White-Taylor philosophise about the vagaries of education in the 1983 staff revue.

Miss Munday and Mrs McGuinness reveal other sides of their personalities in the revue. Mrs McGuinness started 'A' level English Language in the school.

On a trip to Oberammergau, Miss P. Crothers, Mr P. Cowburn and Mr D. Smith enjoy the sunshine. The range of school visits would have astounded the pre-war authorities.

Miss Munday presides over form 2HM in 1983.

Murder in the Cathedral was the play in 1983. Jim Hopcraft was Becket; the three knights are, from left to right: Stephen Truman, Patrick Jennings and Roland Shanks. The priest on the right is Gordon Giles.

The three witches in the 1987 production of *Macbeth* are, from the left: George Thomas, George Rockett, Perrin Sledge.

The under-15 team reached the final of the Lords Taverners' Colts Trophy at Edgbaston. From left to right, back row: Dr S.R. Barker, G. Saunders, S. Ali, D. McNamara, H. Twitchen, T. Clark, M. Taylor, D. Meli, C. Tattersall. Front row: I. Cann, M. Middleton, M. Dodds, J. Skrimshire, P. Shayler, R. Devonport, S. Dutton.

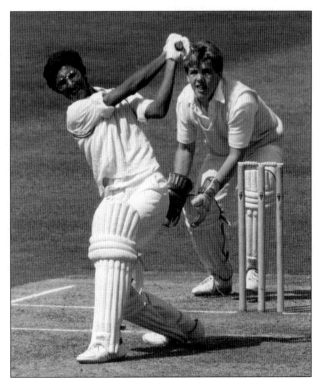

S. Ali, a hockey player, made the top score of fifty-seven in a total of 197 for RGS. Malvern College, however, thanks to two big innings, were 201 for three.

The Sports Hall incorporated a new dining hall and kitchen on the ground floor. In November 1987 the building was officially opened by His Royal Highness the Duke of Gloucester. The Headmaster, R.P. Brown, introduces the Duke to Miss H.R. Munday, Head of Modern Languages, while J.K. Prior, Chairman of the Governors, looks on.

The under-18 National Hockey Champions in 1988. From left to right, back row: Tucker, Nielsen, McAllister, Bambury, Mould, Chandler, Dean. Front row: Hall, S. Ali, Cook, Wyatt, Lane, King, McCauley. Jonathan Wyatt, playing as an under-15 in the team, later played for Great Britain in the Atlanta Olympics and was captain in Sydney 2000.

Three retired Masters take their ease in Prague. From the left: Revd A.J. Skipp, D.G. Jones, E.G. Holmes.

Mr Russel Everett came to teach Physics after leaving Zimbabwe. He started the Electronics courses in the school.

Mr Hussey conducts the Junior Orchestra in the large Music room, with peripatetic teacher R. Griffin in the background.

In 1986 the rugby squad made a tour of Portugal. From left to right, back row: Trobridge, Coppen-Gardner, Miller, Campbell, Pearson, Currie, Eales. Second row: Pond, Clegg, Tapley, Ball, Harrison, Chuter, Cook, Goldstone, McNamara. Front row: Read, P. Smith, A. Welby, Mr Tattersall, Mr D. Stubbs, Mr Gamester, F. Brown, Stone, Baker.

On Miss Munday's trip to Sorrento, from left to right, back row, are: P. Oram, M. Groves, G. Milward, A. Speedy. Front row: J. Cook, T. Channon.

The 1990 First XI had a mixed season, winning six, drawing six and losing three. From left to right, back row: Hall, Dawson, Cartledge. Second row: Woolliams, Harding, L'Estrange, Parker, Chipping, Mr A. Yeates. Front row: Warboys, Garvie, Shaw, Wyatt, Speedy. Matthew Dawson is now a professional rugby player with Northampton and has captained the England rugby team.

The library provision having become overwhelmed by the numbers of boys, especially at Sixth Form level, it was decided to make the Old Hall into a library and Information Technology centre, with provision on a new mezzanine floor for private study. The school was delighted that the Princess of Wales was to open the new library on 6 June 1991. Here, the Princess and Mr R.P. Brown stand either side of the commemorative stone plaque.

Miss Pam Blackwell, the Headmaster's secretary, greets the Princess. Standing in line, from left to right, are Jonathan Preece, recently returned from the Gulf War, and Ted Bradmore, laboratory technician.

From the left: J.K. Prior,
M.J. Moffatt, Her Royal Highness,
I.R. Clark, Mrs J. Clark, R.M. Page,
Mrs M. Page.

Despite tight security, many boys were able to see the royal visitor at close quarters. To the right of the Princess are, from left to right: -?-, Simon Noakes, Oliver Currell and George Rockett, who all smile appreciatively.

Sixth Formers hard at work in the cramped former library, now the Arts centre.

The 1992 drama production was *Amadeus*, for which some publicity pictures were taken at West Wycombe House. On the left is N. Simpson as Salieri, and right is T. Adams as Mozart.

Also in 1992 the twenty-fifth anniversary dinner of the staff soccer team was held. From left to right, back row: N. North, R. Dosser, R. Page, C. Howe. Second row: D. Chamberlain, M. Ball, I. Clark, D. Powell, S. Mason, M. Mill, D. Stone, S. Goldthorpe, P. Gibson, I. Rodger, S. Noyes, E. Wolton, M. Earl, P. Taylor, S. Gamester, J. Cave. Third row: P. Brown, M. Cook, J. Lingard, R.P. Brown, R. File, S. Grundy, M. Moffatt, I. Wilson, R. Stevens. Front row: S. Hussey, S. Box, M. Davies, C. Tattersall, M. Grout, R. Chuter.

The television personality Jan Leeming had a son at RGS and here she is taking part in a Christmas entertainment with P.G. Cowburn. The boys, from left to right, are: O. Rundell, -?-, N. Lindner, W. Village, -?-, -?-, P. Parvin, A. Jackson.

On Mr Brown's retirement in 1993 the Governors held a reception in his honour. From left to right, back row: P.M. Gibson, R. Dixon, B. Peatey, W. Rooke, D. Andrew, J.E. Millbourn, Mr Richards, E.G. Barratt. Second row: I. Gordon, Mr Mawhood, Mrs Mander, Mrs Gibson, D. Chamberlain, G. Knox, Mrs Mawhood, Mrs Knox, Mrs M. Dewar, Mrs Dixon, Mrs Rooke, Mrs Jones, Mrs Andrew, Mrs A. Richards, Mrs Millbourn, Mrs Grant, I. Grant, M. Mander, M. Jones. Front row: Mrs Gordon, F. Secker, -?-, J.K. Prior, Mrs Brown, R.P. Brown, Mrs Prior, G. Ray, Mrs Ray, J. Cook.

The staff of 1993 numbered ninety-seven, including support staff. Mr and Mrs Brown are flanked by the Deputy Headmasters and other senior staff.

In July 1996 the school was presented with a certificate for being 'An outstandingly successful school' by the Secretary of State for Education, Mrs Gillian Shephard. From left to right: A. Bentall, M. Pilgerstorfer, Mr D. Levin (Headmaster), N. Edwards, Mr M. Berry.

The first RGS team to win all of its matches at the Royal Grammar Schools' annual cricket festival is pictured here in 1996. From left to right, back row: Mr W. Phelan, A. Moore, A. Pembroke, D. Wilson, S. Musk, S. Duncombe, K. Guha, Mr M. Davies. Seated: R. Royce, M. Ginn, A. Bentall, G. Watts (captain), D. Moore, S. Grant.

The Navy section of the C.C.F. uses Danesfield Sailing Club near Marlow for much of its work. At the General Inspection, the Inspecting Officer has just come ashore and starts to inspect the cadets. To the immediate left of the Inspecting Officer is Lt T. Claye and to his right Col F.N. Cooper.

In recent years the History and French departments have organised visits to First World War battle sites. Here, in 1997, Mr D. Keysell is addressing a group near Ypres.

The under-15 rugby team won the Daily Mail Cup at Twickenham in 1997. Here Nick Duncombe is being interviewed for Sky Television. He subsequently captained England's 18 group schoolboys and won two caps for the full England team. His sudden death from blood poisoning in February 2003, at age twenty-one, shocked all who knew him.

Fitness training on a 'torture machine' in the Sports Hall.

The new Languages building, named in honour of John Prior, was officially opened by the Duchess of Gloucester in November 1998.

The wide range of languages taught has enabled the school to have 'Language College' status. Mrs Webber is teaching Japanese, watched by the Duchess and Headmaster, Mr David Levin.

The Language block is well equipped with Information Technology facilities. Mr Levin and Miss Munday allow the Duchess, who is Danish, to inspect Gareth Jones's work.

The Science block had to be restructured in 1998 as it was suffering from 'concrete cancer'. The top floor was removed and a new Biology block was built next to it.

On the far left is the new Biology block, and next to it the re-roofed Science block. The new Fraser-Youens boarding house is to the right of the picture.

Fraser-Youens House was officially opened in October 1999. From the left, J.K. Prior, W. Rooke, Chairman of the Governors, and the Lord Lieutenant of Buckinghamshire, Sir Nigel Mobbs. The lectern came from the chapel: John Prior had given generously to the chapel's furnishing in 1960.

The mayor of High Wycombe being weighed at the end of his year of office is Peter Cartwright, mayor from 1990-2000. He was a former pupil at RGS from 1954 to 1960.

Rafiq Raja (at RGS 1970-72), seen here with Councillor Mrs E.M. Barratt, was one of the Old Boys featured at the Millennium Exhibition organised by Mr J. Roebuck, Head of History. Mr Raja writes a regular column in the *Bucks Free Press*.

The exhibition was held in the school library, and here at a reception held for Old Boys are, from the left: Mr I.J. Wilson, Mr Anthony Miles, former editor of the *Daily Mirror*; Michael Zander, Professor of Law at London School of Economics; Mrs Miles.

Mr David Keysell talks to Fergus Walsh, Health and Social Affairs Correspondent for BBC television news. Mr Walsh was at RGS from 1974 to 1980.

Eleven Old Boys were members of staff in 2000. From left to right: Messrs Woolliams, Hollingworth, Noyes, Stone, Clark, Toller, Blyth, Gamester, Willmot, Lewis, Armstrong.

A Geography field trip at Durdle Door, Dorset, in 2000. From left to right, back row: D. Read, M. Harrild, P. Chandler, W. Wachak, P. Connors. Front row: R. Stuart, R. Whyte, S. Burton, A. Waterfall, P. Snowden.

The 2002 drama production was an inspiring performance of *West Side Story*, with the music directed by Mr T. Venvell and the drama by Mr P. Cowburn. Tony (Dominic Townsend) and Maria (Catherine Rice) dance against an authentic-looking New York background.

The under-18 hockey team defeated Kent College to become South-East England Champions in 2002 at Seaford College's ground in Sussex. They lost to Millfield in the national semi-final, though.

124

Speech Day 2002 was enlivened by the school's musicians, conducted by Mr Venvell.

The Bar National Mock Trial Competition, held in November 2002, saw three RGS boys in the final at Oxford Crown Court. From left to right: M. Guttfield, I. Afzal, R. Sanderson.

The RGS team were English Schools Athletics Association Champions in 2002. From left to right, back row: Mr J. Scourfield, J. Blackie, A. Daniels, C. Robinson, P. Rodgers, A. Groom, J. Young, E. Dickson, K. Langley-Hunt, Mr M. Ashby. Front row: R. Bushrod, J. Escobar, B. Collins, T. Hunt, C. Record, M. Robinson, C. Johnstone.

A new mood in the country at large encouraged the school to observe the two-minute silence on 11 November. In 2002 the whole school was able to stand in the Quadrangle for the short ceremony.

School Chaplain Mr Garth Ratcliffe instituted Sixth Form dinners at Pembroke College, Oxford, where the boys could hear good Christian speakers and discuss matters of faith in a congenial atmosphere. From left to right are Chris Kehrhan, Kyle Dickson, Tom Oldnall and James Houston.

In 2003 it was announced that RGS was top of the GCSE League Tables. The Headmaster, T.T. Dingle, is clearly delighted.

Mr Blyth's last Staff Revue – *You're having a staff* – played to packed houses in December 2002. Here the Three Tenors, alias Mr Nick Cousins, Mr John Roebuck, Mr Derek White-Taylor, bid the audience farewell.

FORM OF APPLICATION.

I,

of   hereby desire

the admission of my son,

aged   years on   last, to

the Wycombe Grammar School, to the regulations

of which I agree.

Signed

187

To the Head Master,
    Wycombe Grammar School.

An application form from Revd James Poulter's time. If only it were as simple today!